Celebrating Differences

We All Look
Different

by **Melissa Higgins**

Consulting Editor: Gail Saunders-Smith, PhD

Consultant: Donna Barkman
Children's Literature Specialist and Diversity Consultant
Ossining, New York

CAPSTONE PRESS
a capstone imprint

Pebble Plus is published by Capstone Press,
1710 Roe Crest Drive, North Mankato, Minnesota 56003.
www.capstonepub.com

Library of Congress Cataloging-in-Publication Data
Higgins, Melissa
  We all look different / by Melissa Higgins.
     p. cm.—(Pebble Plus. Celebrating differences)
  Includes bibliographical references and index.
  Summary: "Simple text and full-color photos celebrate differences in appearances"—Provided by publisher.
  ISBN 978-1-4296-7576-5 (library binding)—ISBN 978-1-4296-7890-2 (paperback)
  1. Individual differences in children—Juvenile literature. 2. Individual differences—Juvenile literature. 3. Human
physiology—Juvenile literature. I. Title.

  BF723.I56H54 2012
  155.2'2—dc23   2011036743

Editorial Credits
Jeni Wittrock, editor; Gene Bentdahl, designer; Svetlana Zhurkin, media researcher; Kathy McColley, production
    specialist; Marcy Morin, studio scheduler; Sarah Schuette, photo stylist

Photo Credits
Capstone Studio: Karon Dubke, cover; Dreamstime: James Blinn, 9; iStockphoto: Aldo Murillo, 20–21, Blend_Images,
7, Daniel Laflor, 5, Nina Shannon, 1; Photolibrary: Tim Jones, 19; Shutterstock: Distinctive Images, 15, GWImages, 17,
Monkey Business Images, 10–11, Rob Hainer, 13

Note to Parents and Teachers

The Celebrating Differences series supports national social studies standards related to
individual development and identity. This book describes and illustrates differences in
appearance. The images support early readers in understanding the text. The repetition of
words and phrases helps early readers learn new words. This book also introduces early readers
to subject-specific vocabulary words, which are defined in the Glossary section. Early readers
may need assistance to read some words and to use the Table of Contents, Glossary, Read
More, Internet Sites, and Index sections of the book.

Printed in the United States of America in Stevens Point, Wisconsin.
072013   007586R

Table of Contents

I Like How I Look

How we look is one thing that
makes you, *you*—and me, *me*.
I like who I am. I like the
things that make me unique.

We Look Different

My friends have cinnamon skin,

peach skin, and chocolate skin.

We are all shapes and sizes.

Summer is our favorite time
of year. The sun gives us more
freckle power!

My hair is curly and yours is straight. We both like going to the library.

11

I am short and quick. I am
the fastest runner on my team.

We Dress Differently

The things I wear tell a story
about me. Orange is sunny
and happy, just like me.

My glasses help me see.
Grandma says my glasses
are picture frames for
my shining, brown eyes.

My braces help me get into
the game. I love to play
and practice hard.

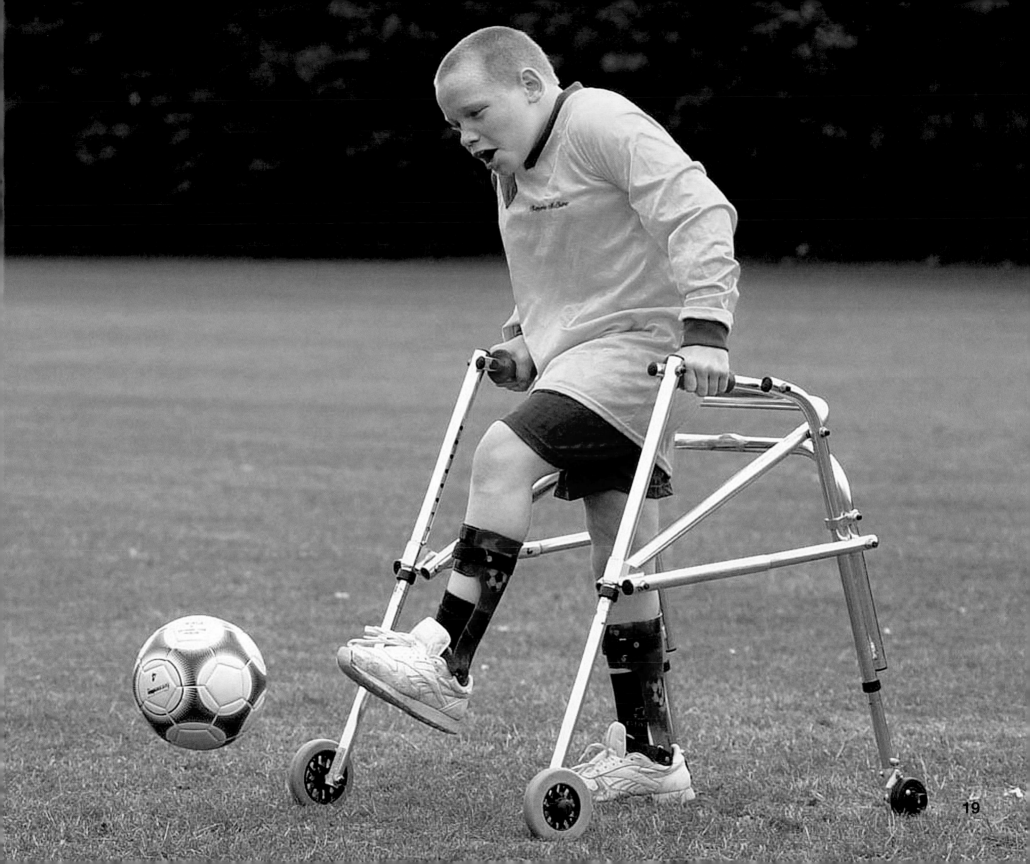

We Like Being Different

Differences make life
interesting. We are each
one of a kind.

 Glossary

brace—a frame worn around part of your body to support it

frame—a border that surrounds something, like a picture frame

freckle—a small, light brown spot on a person's skin

unique—one of a kind

Read More

Fox, Mem. *Whoever You Are.* San Diego: Harcourt Brace, 2006.

Parr, Todd. *It's Okay to Be Different.* New York: Little, Brown Books for Young Readers, 2009.

Tyler, Michael. *The Skin You Live In.* Chicago: Chicago Children's Museum, 2005.

Internet Sites

FactHound offers a safe, fun way to find Internet sites related to this book. All of the sites on FactHound have been researched by our staff.

Here's all you do:

Visit *www.facthound.com*

Type in this code: 9781429675765

 **Super-cool stuff!** Check out projects, games and lots more at **www.capstonekids.com**

Index

Word Count: 144
Grade: 1
Early-Intervention Level: 17